How to Be a Happy Husband

A MARITAL-WISDOM KIT

Based on 50+ Years of Marriage and 90+ Years of Life Experience

Lee Evers

ILLUSTRATIONS BY THE AUTHOR

How to Be a Happy Husband: A Marital-Wisdom Kit, based on 50+ years of marriage and 90+ years of life experience. Copyright © 2017 by Lee Evers. All rights reserved.

Printed in the United States of America.

No part of this publication may be reproduced, distributed or transmitted in any form or by any means, including photocopying, recording, or other electronic or mechanical methods, without the prior written permission of the publisher, except in the case of brief quotations embodied in critical reviews and certain other noncommercial uses permitted by copyright law. For permission requests, contact the publisher, addressed "Attention: Permissions Coordinator," by means of the email below.

Happy Ever After Publications
An imprint of Rose Press
www.rosepress.com
rosepressbooks@yahoo.com

Illustration: Lee Evers
Editing and Book Production: Naomi Rose
Book Layout ©2017, BookDesignTemplates.com

Ordering Information:
Quantity sales. Special discounts are available on quantity purchases by organizations, associations, and others. For details, contact the "Special Sales Department" by emailing rosepressbooks@yahoo.com.

How to Be a Happy Husband: A Marital-Wisdom Kit/ Lee Evers —1st ed.
ISBN 978-0-9816278-7-8

Contents

Introduction 1

1. Upon Rising, Remember to: 12
2. Once a Week 14
3. Before Going to Bed 16
4. Out and About 18
   When Driving 18
   When Walking 20
   At Gatherings 22
5. While Watching TV 24
6. At Mealtime 26
7. Pleasant Conversation 28
8. Compromise Can Bring You Closer 36
   Entertainment 36
   Trips 38
   Food Preparation 38
   House Cleaning 38
9. Money Is Very Important When You're a Couple 40
   Negotiating Important Expenditures 40
   When There Are Differences in Earnings 44
   Helping a Child, Friend, or Relative 44
   Charities 44
10. Mutual Interests 46
11. Going without Her 48
12. When Your Mate Is Sick or Tired 50
13. Medical Matters 52

14. Driving in the Car Together 54

15. When You Have Guests Coming 56

16. Around the House 58

17. When Shopping for Food 60

18. Clothes Shopping for Her 62

19. Phone Your Mate at Work 64

20. On Occasion, Remember to Tell Her 66

21. Never in Her Presence 68

22. Sex 70

23. Romancing 72

    More Romancing 74

    When Romancing 76

24. Visiting People 78

25. Emotions 80

26. Just for Fun 84

27. Holidays 88

Conclusion 97

Acknowledgments 98

About the Author 99

Dedication

There's no question that my unbelievable wife, Lil, created most of the pertinent material that is in this kit. She provided the care and love that only a near-perfect wife can accomplish. I used this to help you guys.

A Note to My Readers:

Before using this kit, keep this important information in mind:

If you are unhappy in your marriage, immediately seek marriage counseling. Ask relatives, friends, your doctor, your spiritual leader, or a governing agency in this field to assist you in locating the competent help you require to save your marriage.

If your marriage is loveless—physically, sexually, spiritually, and emotionally—and the counseling does not help: get a divorce.

But read this book first. It may give you the boost you need to take the other steps to become *a happy husband*.

Introduction

If you're a guy, there's a good chance that you can have a happier marriage. The purpose of this book is for you to become contented in your life with a woman, and this will surely make you happier.

This book is based on roughly 90 years of wide experience. The idea is for you to use each section of the kit when and where it suits your needs. Using this kit will make an immense difference in winning your gal's love, attention, and sexual desire. It's designed for easy use.

The suggestions on becoming a happy husband are laid out for you in boxes. Please make the necessary mental note by snipping out those that are relevant with a scissors - or copying them onto an index card (or even into your smart phone, if you use one). That way, you can have them handy, and even rework them to fit the needs of your own situation and relationship.

Remember these things about your mate:
- She looks inward. She wants your respect, and your admiration for her appearance, her behavior, and her conversation.
- She wants you to think highly of her ideas, her taste in movies, TV, books, magazines, and newspapers.
- Your mate wants you to approve of her.

Always know that your genitals are driven to keep the human species alive. Btu we are no longer cavemen. It's very important to be aware of how the female differs from us guys. Notice your mate! How her eyes and mouth move. How she turns her head, uses her hands, and expresses herself. Her movements and expressions are probably different from yours. And this should teach us not to expect our mates to grasp what we are all about. They see us as strange creatures!

By knowing that we're different, you can more readily be sympathetic toward your mate and understand her. Learn to listen carefully when your mate speaks, and try to be accepting.

Before you go to sleep at night, remember that your gal is rarely as interested in having sex as you are. It is smart to indicate to her that your interest is in *her*, and not just her vagina. Try to show her how much you want to be her real mate. The activities that follow in this kit are actually ways to show her that you want to do this.

It is important to find fun activities that you and your mate can do together. Apartness will not add to your love for each other. There will be exceptions to this rule, but for most of the time, learn what your mate enjoys doing.

When you do the following activities with your mate, take your attention off yourself and put it on her. What is she thinking, feeling, and doing?

A Chapter from My Story

In order for you, a husband, to have a really HAPPY MARRIAGE, consider my 50-plus years of great contentment in my marriage to a wonderful woman, Lil. I've been blessed with a deeply caring wife. She tells me she adores me. That's the highest accord I've ever gotten in my life.

Whenever we had some difficulty, we calmly discussed whatever was wrong and agreed upon a workable solution. Problem solved.

To let you know where I'm coming from, I'd like to touch on my background:

My mother died of gallstones at age 28, the week of my first birthday. So I was raised by a small contingent of close relatives (grandparents, two aunts, one of their lovers, and my depressed dad) who lavished love on me to compensate for my loss. And in the small Bronx ghetto, everyone knew each other, and almost all of my friends' parents (mostly mothers) singled me out to show they wanted to help make up for my not having my mother.

Being immersed with mainly female caretakers, I grasped their natures early on, loved them immensely, and learned how to repay their endless kindnesses. I gained a unique perspective about women that has enabled me to understand them in ways that most men don't.

Understanding a Woman

Understanding a woman and meeting her needs is entirely different from either placating or dominating a woman.

Part of understanding a woman is dealing with her criticism. Here's a news flash for you! The woman in your life is probably going to criticize you. Don't let the criticism injure your self-esteem. A big part of being a man is an impenetrable, unshakeable belief in yourself. *Listen* to the criticism. *Think* about it. Maybe it is valid, maybe it isn't. Valid criticism should refer to something you *do*, not who you *are*. "The dishes you washed are still dirty"—that may be valid criticism. "You are stupid"—that's not valid criticism.

Never let that criticism, valid or invalid, interfere with your sense of wellbeing. Never let that criticism cause an unnecessary argument. The best response to criticism often is, "I'll think about what you said." And as you think about it, retain a sense of well-being. Always keep that sense of well-being in your marriage as you undertake to understand your mate.

Women are different from guys. A woman is basically soft, seeking a man's interest, his protection, and his interaction with her concerns. That's far from what men want. They seek sex first, food, and comfort. Their mate is someone who is supposed to provide these things. The trick is to learn how to accept all they give, and to return to them what they need. The rewards for that are immense.

A Happy Marriage Makes Good Things Happen

The really astounding thing about a happy marriage is how it affects so many people. My wife, Lil, and I, looking back, constantly are amazed at our seemingly endless supply of kindness, care, cooperation, gifts, and help from so many people. We have to assume it is due to our ability to love each other that other people recognize about us. They reach out to be part of it. They simply want to add their particular effort to our loving relationship with each other. There is simply no other way to explain it.

Here are a few examples of this.

- We had no funds to get to Mexico for our divorce from previous mates. At work, a salesman friend of mine, Sidney Marks, asked, "How much do you need?" I told him. He wrote a check. He wasn't even a close friend; he just wanted to help.

- Right after Lil and I got married, we decided to buy an old house that we liked. The problem was, we had no money in the bank. My cousin May's husband asked his mother to lend us the down-payment amount. She did. A mystery, I tell ya.

- An old friend in the furniture business, Natie, knew both Lil and me when we were school kids. Years later, I met Natie by accident in New York City. I told him that Lil and I were newly marriage and strapped for cash in an old house we'd just put a down payment on. I also mentioned that we needed furniture. He immediately dispatched a truck full of new furniture to us and told me, "Pay me back whenever you have the money." I eventually did. Call it luck?

- Years later, my wife's sister and her very close cousin both left us a lot of money in their wills. It sure was a huge surprise. We knew of no reason to receive such sizable sums of money. The only reason: They loved my wife.

- A couple who lived across the entire country from us did an amazing thing: they rented a car for us, gave us tickets to a three-day jazz concert, and loaned us their condominium in the same town. What a beautiful gift! They must have liked us a lot.

- A single man, quite well off, has repeatedly given us large cash sums of money for our birthdays and anniversaries. He also invites us to stay with him in his most attractive and huge home, complete with swimming pool, gymnasium, and basketball court. Call it luck?

- We have numerous friends all over the country who offer us a huge amount of care, and endless offerings of all kinds, to show their love. They rent motel rooms for us, take us to expensive restaurants, pay for our airfare, and throw parties for us. Why do they do all these wonderful things? We have to conclude that it's our happy marriage. That has been a magnet that's pulled in all kinds of wonderful things from other people.

HOW TO BE A HAPPY HUSBAND

I've created this kit to help *you* have a happy marriage. This kit gives you hundreds of ways to show your wife a part of your nature that you may have overlooked. This kit will show you a million ways to express your appreciation for the good things you wife does for you.

Here's an example: After my wife serves me breakfast, I might say, "This orange tastes so good. Where did you buy it? Darling, this hot cereal is delicious, I love how you make it so smooth." And so on.

So thank your wife for what she does for you. If you haven't been doing this so far, try it out. Go ahead, feller, try being a real partner.

This kit can help. You'll become a happy husband.

Chapter 1

Upon Rising, Remember to:

Hug her briefly.	Hold her to you very closely.	Admire her hair.
Touch her.	Kiss her.	Praise her scent.
Caress her.	Admire what she is wearing.	Tell her how much you hate to leave her when you go to work.

Chapter 2

Once a Week:

On pretty paper, write your wife a note. (Buy some at the stationary store or department store, or decorate the edges of white paper with bright-colored pencils, pens, or crayons, or glue pretty strips of paper at the edges.) Address each one differently, as follows:

Darling, I love you so much. You are everything I want.	Sweetheart, each day is beautiful because I share it with you.	Beloved, without you I would be brokenhearted. You brighten my life.	Honey Bunch, you're so much fun. Never, never change.	Adorable, you bring music and flowers into my life. Stay as sweet as you are.
Honey, before you I had nothing. You've enriched me. I'm just a lucky man.	Precious, I'm so fortunate to spend my time with you. You thrill me and fulfill me.	My love, I kiss your soft fingers in my dreams. So let me do that now.	Baby, whenever I look at you, I get an increased heartbeat.	Gorgeous, did you know that every time I look at you, I want to embrace and kiss you? Well, you know it now.

Chapter 3

Before Going to Bed:

Become a participant in making the bedroom more tidy and appealing, and in appreciating your wife once you're both in bed, so that she will see your willingness to help in different ways. This is often overlooked by guys and left entirely to the woman. Be the unusual guy. It will win you points. Try some of the examples that follow.

Help remove and fold up the bed covers. Straighten the pillows and sheets.	Give her a kiss, gently.	Admire your mate's sleepwear and body.
Ask if there is anything that has been overlooked but may be worth discussing before going to sleep.	Once in bed, gently embrace your mate.	Tell your mate, "I love you."

Chapter 4

Out and About

When you're out and about together, keep in mind these various ways you can win her affection and attention.

When Driving:

Hold her hand.	Put your hand on her knee.
Point out interesting things as you pass them by.	Place your hand on the back of her neck.

HOW TO BE A HAPPY HUSBAND • 19

When Walking:

Put her arm inside of yours.	Ask if the pace is all right for her.	Point out anything you think she may be interested in (for example, trees, passing cars, signs, people) so you can both share the experience.
Tell her how much you enjoy walking together.	Ask her what is the best route to take to where you are going.	If there is no conversation, think of things to discuss, such as: (1) Name 10 places in the world starting with the letter K. (2) Name 10 state capitols. (3) Give 10 names for women starting with the letter L.

At Gatherings:

Whisper in her ear how nicely she is dressed.	Keep an eye on her. If she is alone, join her to show a deep interest. (If she prefers to be alone, she will say so.)	Ask if she's enjoying the gathering. If she's bored, offer to leave early. And if you are bored, tell her; perhaps you both will want to leave early.
Tell her how you like her looks.	If you meet an interesting person, introduce that person to your mate.	If you're enjoying the gathering, tell the host. You will be invited to return another time.
Bring her a drink or some food.	Ask her opinion about the furniture and general décor.	After leaving, tell your mate how pleased you are to have shared the experience with her.

Chapter 5

While Watching TV

Hold her hand.	Ask if you can bring her a drink or a snack.	Ask her for her reaction to the show. Ask if she wants to hear your reaction to the show.
Ask if she would prefer to watch a different show.	After the show, ask if she enjoyed it.	Kiss her tenderly once you close the TV set.

Chapter 6

At Mealtime

Set the table.	Toast the bread for her.	Tell her you're glad she serves healthy food.
Ask how her day went.	Tell her what has been happening where you work.	Tell her you love the food she makes.
Talk about a recent TV show or movie you watched together.	Clear off the table when dinner is over, and do the dishes.	Sweep her in your arms and tell her you adore her.

Chapter 7

Pleasant Conversation

Strike up a conversation with your mate. When feasible, share her interests. Ask her personal questions and listen attentively. It's important to do this, because a relationship without stimulating conversation is no fun for anyone. Here are some conversation starters.

"Tell me about…"

A food you enjoy.	A favorite subject in school.	A hobby or interest you have.
What job you liked the best.	The person you admire most.	Something you wish for.

"Tell me about your…"

Mother	Father	Brothers and sisters
Aunts and uncles	Nieces and nephews	Cousins
Teachers	Grandparents	Friends

"Tell me about your favorite…"

Movies	TV shows	Plays
Authors	Radio shows	Magazines or newspapers
Music	Actors	Art
Websites	Podcasts	Facebook pages

"Tell me how you feel about…"

Homosexuality	Mate swapping	Masturbation
Sex change	Infidelity	Inter-marriage, both racial and religious
Illegal drug use	Alcoholism	Gun regulation

And if you want to talk about things more deeply:

What were your dreams for yourself, as a child?	What did you like to do, as a child?
What do you find fulfilling, now?	Is there something you want to explore or do in the next phase of your life that you're not currently doing?

Tell me about your memories of…"

Places you worked	People you worked with/for	Places you lived
Places you traveled to	People you knew years ago	Feelings of belonging
Your first boyfriend	Experiences in nature	When we first were courting
Your favorite color	A show or movie we both saw a long time ago	Happy times

"Tell me about your memories of school days…"

Preschool	Elementary school	Middle school
High school	College	Graduate school
Vocational training	Current educational pursuits	Favorite teachers

All memories are important.

Things you can do together if you're bored:

| Play the "cities" game. Pick a letter. Each of you name a city beginning with that letter until you run out of cities. | Each of you try counting backwards from 100 in 7s: 93, 86, etc. | Pick a letter. Name 10 women's first names beginning with that letter. | While driving, count the number of Toyotas, Fords, Chevys, Hondas, etc. See which car wins! |

"How about your interests in the creative area?"

Your favorite museum experience	The type of art you most admire	Artists you think are outstanding
Your favorite sculpture	Your thoughts on censorship of art	Ballet
Poetry	Your thoughts on using tax money to support art	Music

"Some creative things we could do together…"

| Cook | Play music | Sing |

You can come up with some creative ideas of your own!

Chapter 8

Compromise Can Bring You Closer

If you want to do one thing and she wants to do another—do neither. Instead, pick something you both would like to do. Or first do what she'd like, then what you'd like.

Entertainment:

Here are some examples in the area of entertainment:

TOPIC	SHE	YOU	THE COMPROMISE
TV	She likes drama, love stories, and health shows.	You prefer sports, action, and reality shows.	First watch a drama, then sports. Or select a show you'd both like.
Movies	She likes drama, love stories, and documentaries.	You like action movies, thrillers, and sports movies.	Make a list of movies you'd both like, and see one together. (This discussion could bring you closer.)

Trips:

SHE	YOU	THE COMPROMISE
She wants to go one place for a vacation.	You want to go another place.	You could take separate trips. Or perhaps you can find a trip you *both* would like so you don't need to be separated. Or one of you chooses a destination this time, and the other one gets to choose next time.

Food Preparation:

SHE	YOU	THE COMPROMISE
"The foods I prepare cost more, because they are healthier."	"Let's find foods that are OK to eat, but cheaper."	Buy half the food your way, and half the food her way. Or, she continues to prepare healthier meals and you come up with different ways to pay for them. Or, you agree to grow some vegetables and herbs in the garden or on a windowsill.

House Cleaning:

SHE	YOU	THE COMPROMISE
"I hate housework, and I'm raising the kids and holding down a job."	"I hate housework, and I'm raising the kids and holding down a job."	Divide the work up 50/50. Each partner selects the housework that they don't hate as much. Offer words and gestures of mutual empathy for each other's working and raising the kids.

Chapter 9

Money Is Very Important When You're a Couple

After sex, money is the most important element requiring agreement in a couple's life.

The first thing to decide is how to divide the income. Both must agree on whatever is spent. Keep talking until an agreement is reached. A compromise can be either:

| Agreeing | OR | Choosing equal alternatives |
|---|---|---|//

If you both agree, then you can proceed.

If you simply cannot agree, then work out a plan where each of you gets what you need on a separate basis.

Negotiating Important Expenditures:

Let's say you need two cars—one for you to get to work, and one for your mate to get to her work. Both of your current cars have over 100,000 miles on them and are unreliable. You want to take $30,000 out of the bank to get a new car for you and one for your mate. She says "Yes" to this. *This is compromise #1, Agreeing.*

Now, let's say your mate changes her mind and says, "$30,000 is too much to spend on automobiles." You say, "OK, how much do you think we can spend?" She says, "$20,000." You say, "OK, we'll each take $10,000 and buy any kind of used car each of us wants." That would be *compromise #2, Choosing Equal Alternatives.*

Or here's another example:

A guy may want a new car, while his mate wants a bedroom renovation. A compromise *must* be negotiated early on. Here's an example of a negotiation:

Joe: "A new car is necessary for me to impress my customers at work."

Mary: "Our bedroom is so depressing. I hate sleeping in it each night."

Joe: "We only have $15,000 in savings. Enough for a pretty good car."

Mary: "If I'm not happy when we go to bed, you won't be very happy the next morning. That won't help your sales, no matter how nice your car is."

Joe: "Good point. How about we'll do the bedroom renovation this year, and then we'll start saving for a new car."

Mary (with a smile): "OK."

When there are differences in earnings:

If one partner earns more than the other, basically share whatever earnings come into the marriage on a 50/50 basis.	After either of you gets what you want, regardless of income differences the one who "gave in" should regularly *tease* the "winner."

Helping a child, friend, or relative:

Thoroughly discuss this before the favor is granted. By agreeing on exactly how much money, what gift, or how much time will be given, a lot of strife can be avoided.

Charities:

You each may have your own favorite charities.	Be sure each partner is allowed an equal amount to donate.

Chapter 10

Mutual Interests

It is important to find fun activities that you and your mate can do together. Apartness will not add to your love for each other.

There will be exceptions to this rule. For example, maybe you love basketball and your mate hates it. Or she loves ballet, and you hate it. The solution: now and then, you go to a basketball game without your mate, or she goes to the ballet without you. That's a good thing now and then.

But for most of the time, learn what your mate enjoys doing. Pick an activity she enjoys that you already enjoy now, or could learn to like. Here are some possibilities:

Dancing. Find out where local dancing takes place — clubs, restaurants, dancing schools.

Music. Find out what concerts will be available in the near future. Find out what type of music your mate likes. Suggest going to a concert that your mate would love and you could enjoy at least a little.

Stage plays, or movies at a movie theater. Pick one you'd both be interested in. A play that you and your mate have seen together will become an excellent subject for the two of you to discuss.

TV shows or DVDs at home. Together, watch what you both like. If you want to watch a football game, and she wants to watch a cooking show, tape them and watch them without the other's presence. Or for TV shows, you can switch between shows during the commercials.

Restaurants. Only eat where you're both content.

Friends. See only the ones you both enjoy.

Relatives. Here, you compromise. You visit her relatives with her, and she visits your with you. *Be a sport.* If you're lucky, you may even come to like the relatives.

Chapter 11

Going without Her

When you have reason to go somewhere without your mate, keep in mind that she may resent it. She may feel lonely or abandoned, or like she wants to go with you. Discuss it with her, first. Find a solution that is agreeable to both of you. Here are some examples:

WHAT YOU WANT	SOLUTIONS FOR THE TWO OF YOU
You want to watch a sports event with some other guys.	You and your mate decide that you'll watch the sports event with the guys. The next day, you and your mate will go to a movie.
You want to go to the gym for a workout.	You and your mate decide that she will join you at the gym.
You want to visit a buddy who is sick in bed.	You and your mate decide that you will visit your buddy alone, and later in the day you and your mate will go to a neat restaurant.
You want to play tennis. Your mate wants to go bowling.	You and your mate decide to play miniature golf.
You want to go to a trade show.	You and your mate decide that you will both go to the trade show.
You want to go to a job-related lecture.	You and your mate decide that you'll go to the lecture and she'll stay home and read. After the lecture, you surprise her with a bouquet of flowers.

Chapter 12

When Your Mate Is Sick or Tired

Ask her, "Shall I phone the doctor?"	Ask her, "Do you need medicine?"	Sit next to her and put your arm around her.	Massage her back.
Tell her, "Go ahead and lie down. Here's a blanket."	Lower the shade. Ask, "Would you like the lights off?"	Ask, "Would you like to watch anything on TV?"	Ask, "Hungry? What would you like me to get you?"
Kiss her forehead.	Let her know how important she is to you.	Bring her a glass of water.	Ask, "What do you need?" and then let her tell you.

Chapter 13

Medical Matters

Sometimes your wife may have a medical problem. If so, keep a pad of paper handy and when she mentions what's wrong, *write it down*. It could be diabetes, high blood pressure, or, more likely, a condition with a very technical name. If you have written it down, you can Google it and find out information about her condition. The point is not only to help her in the ways you can, but also to show her how deeply you care for her.

Be sure to offer to go to her medical appointments with her, even if it means losing income.	Drive. Let her rest in the car.	Offer her your hand when you leave the car, in case she is hurting, tired, or ill.	Go with her to the examination room. Listen carefully to everything that the health professional says.
On the way home, buy necessary prescriptions or other medical needs.	At home, assist her to a chair, couch, or bed.	Get her something to eat or drink.	Discuss the visit with her to see if the two of your agree on what has taken place.

Be sure to write down what medications she is taking, and her doctors' phone numbers. Discuss her condition with her doctors. Take notes. Later, refer to these notes in a supportive manner.

Chapter 14

Driving in the Car Together

Thank her if she notices that you're going too fast. Who wants a speeding ticket?	Ask her for help with driving directions.	Ask if she wants to stop for a snack.	Thank her if she notices anything important on the dashboard (like being low on gas).
Ask if the car temperature is OK for her.	Ask her what she wants to hear on the radio or CD.	Ask her, "Are you enjoying this road?"	Tell her how much you love her being with you.

Chapter 15

When You Have Guests Coming

Pitching in to get things ready when you have guests coming will really make your mate feel appreciated and supported. She'll be glad for your active participation.

Mark the date on the calendar.	Make up the bed for the guests. Save your mate the time and effort.	Vacuum the house, including the guest room.	Talk with your mate about what food and drink to buy.

HOW TO BE A HAPPY HUSBAND • 57

I

Chapter 16

Around the House

If you work and your wife does not:
Help as much as you can.

If you both have outside jobs:
Do 50% of the housework.

If your wife is the chief cook:
Perhaps at mealtime, you could:

Cut fruit. Pour water.	Set the table.
Put leftover food away.	Wash dishes.

Chapter 17

When Shopping for Food

Go with her, when possible. (Or even go on your own.)

You could:

Make a shopping list.	Be sure you have cash, check, or credit card.
Keep the receipt in case an item needs to be returned.	Carry the heaviest packages into your home.

Chapter 18

Clothes Shopping for Her

It can make a woman feel special when her mate wants to come along and help her shop for clothes. Be sure to make the most of the opportunity!

Ask if she wants you to accompany her. If so, let her know you're interested!	Encourage her to buy what she needs.
Help her make her selections. Give her your honest opinion on each item. (If you really don't care for a particular item, explain what you believe is a better choice.)	Point out attractive items that she may have overlooked.
Suggest other stores.	Compliment her on her taste and price sense. (If the price is *way* too high, tell her so nicely.)
If her choice is a bit more costly than expected, tell her you will find a way to cover the price.	Tell her it's fun to go shopping for her clothing.

Chapter 19

Phone Your Mate at Work

If possible,* always call her:

in the morning,

at lunchtime,

in the afternoon,

and

shortly before you leave work.**

Ask her:

"Is there anything I should pick up?"	"Anything you want me to do when I get home?"	"Do you want to eat out?"	"How was your day?"
"Is there someone we'll be meeting?"	"Should we watch TV, or should I pick up a movie?"	"Do you know what a great mate you are?"	"Do you know that I love you?"

---

* If your job allows. If you can do it three times a day, that's terrific.

** Even if you work from home!

Chapter 20

On Occasion, Remember to Tell Her:

"Your meals are so delicious. Thank you very much."	"It's always a delight to come into my lovely home. You do such a great job."
"Don't think I overlook all those great things you buy for us."	"You're so good at arranging where we go for fun."
"I'm so lucky you have such wonderful relatives."	"Thanks to you, we've made so many good friends."
"I'm blessed to have you help me take care of my health the way you do."	"I don't forget all the efforts you make to keep me content and happy."

Chapter 21

Never in Her Presence:

Nap	Play cards, games, or crossword puzzles
Scribble or draw	Make a phone call
Read a magazine, newspaper, or book	Work at your computer
Watch TV	Walk away without letting her know

Acknowledge her presence. Don't just disappear into a diversion.
Because you don't want your mate to feel ignored.

HOW TO BE A HAPPY HUSBAND • 69

Chapter 22

Sex

The prime reason you got married is that you were sexually attracted to a woman. If you want to be happy, you have to find ways to keep alive, and even improve, the original sexual gratification that you found in your mate.

Recognize that a woman is *internally* constructed. Her sexual equipment is on the *inside*. She is therefore more concerned about her feelings. A man may be attractive to her with his good looks, but most often she will seek one who reminds her of the personal qualities of her dad, grandpa, uncle, brother, or even a teacher.

A man is *externally* constructed. His sexual equipment is on the *outside*. A man looks at a woman and becomes sexually excited. When he's aroused, he wants to have intercourse. But a woman: she will not be aroused simply by looking at a man. Her sexual equipment is inside. That equipment is farther away. It takes longer to get there. Got it?

To make a woman sexually aroused, the man has to find ways to reach the *internal* woman. First he has to connect with her feelings before he can even think about having sex. To connect to the internal woman, praise the outer woman. Praise her shape, her size, her speech, her walk, her skin tone, her shoes, her athletic or buxom figure. Point out her warmth, sense of humor, clarity, and above all else, her caring about you. Be sure to praise her for something real! Let her know you are attracted to her for all these things.

Chapter 23

Romancing

Always remember that for men, the sex act is to quickly unload their sperm inside a woman. The woman, conversely, has to take the sperm into her. This is a more delicate operation. So whenever possible, look at your mate and say or do some thing endearing, like this:

"Your eyes are so beautiful."	"Your lips are so delicious."
"Your skin is so soft to touch."	"May I hold your hand?"
Simply kiss her fingers, one by one.	Kiss her ears. Blow gently into each one.
Hold her head close to your chest.	Stroke her body gently.

More Romancing:

From my personal observation, I find that women usually do want marriage, children, and a warm, loving husband. It fulfills one of humankind's basic needs—to add to the tribe.

Don't count only on your looks or your clothing. Never look a woman over. She will read that as something unclean, as if you were only after her body. Arouse her in many other ways.

When you have found her to be amenable to your physical advances, realize that a woman needs at least eighteen minutes of foreplay before your entry into her womb, whereas a man takes only sixty seconds to come.

So take it slow. Notice what she likes, and keep doing it. Don't start taking off her clothes until you're sure she is aroused.

Take her hand.	Stroke her lower arm.
Stroke her upper arm.	Look in her eyes with adoration.
Hold her hand in yours.	Touch her shoulders.
Kiss her fingers.	Blow very gently into her ear.

HOW TO BE A HAPPY HUSBAND • 75

When Romancing:

Use this list when you have sex. Do everything carefully, with consideration for your mate's feelings. Act slowly. Leave a lot of time between each action.

Kiss her gently.	Use your tongue very lightly to brush her lips.
Touch each breast very carefully. Her breasts are highly sensitive, and respond to your hands.	Introduce your tongue into her mouth slowly, letting your mate react.
Praise her breasts' beauty and loveliness.	Kiss her breasts very gently. Suck the nipples with care.
Gently, touch her knees. Rub them. Explore the area tenderly.	Move your fingers along her thighs, slowly.

Once you place one finger in her vagina, seek the spot she most relates to. Do this by moving your finger in all the areas it can slowly reach. Your mate will respond when you locate it and gently massage it. After that, you both can figure out what's enjoyable.

Chapter 24

Visiting People

Usually, friends or acquaintances are closer either to you or to your mate. If it is you, be sure to keep your mate near you during the visit so she will not feel unsure of herself or of being completely accepted by *your* friends. If she does start mingling with others, then feel free to mingle, yourself. If, on the other hand, they are *her* friends, always make an effort with them by:

Asking for their names:	Mentioning some association, like:	Here, the idea is to become interested in these folks by asking questions like:
To remember a name, always PICTURE something connected to the name. For example: a. *Marilyn*: See a couple getting married. b. *Joanna*: Visualize a banana. c. *Jessica*: Picture a chest of drawers.	*Hannah*: "I had a friend in high school with your name, but I always made the mistake of calling her 'Anna.'" *Lucille*: "Like the TV actress, Lucille Ball." *Charlie*: "I'll remember your name because Charlie Chaplin comes to mind."	a. "Do you live around here? Have you always lived here, or did you move from somewhere else? Where? Kansas? Oh, I liked Kansas." b. "Do you work? What do you do? My nephew, John, works in that field." c. "How did you become friendly with my mate?"

Ask about the person's house, family background, children, and future plans. People you don't know will LIKE YOU if you do this. Act interested in them!

Chapter 25

Emotions

There is a hidden emotional factor you should consider: I believe that all our emotions are housed in the chest area. Every time you get a feeling, perhaps you'll notice that it emanates from that area of the body. Our emotions are very powerful and can easily be the engine that runs us. After all, for 40,000 years as modern humans, we did incorporate the 4,500,000 years of our ape-past history. We can be ape-like, emotionally. But our human emotions also can elevate us to the highest level, enabling us to use them for our best behavior and improve our lives and those of the people we care for. So by using our huge, relatively new, vast brainpower, we can more intelligently deal with the wide variety of emotions we constantly feel.

Think of your emotions as tools in a toolbox. An emotion can help your relationship with your mate or hurt it, depending on the situation. You need to be aware of what emotion you're feeling. Otherwise, you won't be able to use that emotion to help improve your relationship with your mate. Consider how to use these emotions effectively:

Love: The total giving of yourself.	Affection: The need to give and receive it.	Joy: Feeling great happiness.
Inspiration: Inner excitement about some idea.	Compassion: A tenderness for someone.	Tenderness: Wanting to comfort someone.

Yet negative emotions also can come up in a relationship. If this happens, put some attention into turning the negative aspects around. For example:

Avarice: The need to acquire wealth and power—but only by never hurting anyone as you attempt it.	Hatred: The urge to despise. Recognize its negativity and always try to overcome it.	Envy: Wanting what someone else has—but deeply question your feelings.
Fear: The inability to face a person or situation. Be courageous.	Anxiety: Being uncertain. Reflect on what is causing it.	Stress: Worry about a situation. See if you can find a way to relax about it.

Emotions are the key to a happy marriage. So let's stop and think this matter out deeply.

The emotions listed above entail personal matters that may widen your own perspective. Here are some examples from my own experience.

1. **Avarice:** At Mattel Toy Company, my compatriots sought wealth, primarily. I noticed a lack of more meaningful understanding and chose not to associate with these executives.
2. **Hatred:** I hated the owner of a clothing firm I worked with. Developing painful arthritis in my back, I sought a male psychotherapist who held out the lid of a large metal garbage can and told me to hit it. I did, powerfully—and my pain vanished.
3. **Envy:** I was enthralled by a friend's wife, envying him such a prize. He told me to stop ogling her. I stopped.
4. **Anxiety:** Waiting for a call-back on a job I wanted, I was unable to sleep and became reclusive. However, when I thought it over carefully, I realized that if this job did not come through, I would look elsewhere. My anxiety was over.

Perhaps these examples could help you realize how to deal with your *own* personal emotional needs. That will make your marriage a happier one.

Chapter 26

Just for Fun

Over a weekend or holiday:

Pretend you are in a foreign country. Use only the bedroom, as if it is a hotel room. Do not accept or make any phone calls. When you go out, never go anyplace you have been before. It would be a really amusing experience!

Visit all the bars, briefly—not to get drunk, but to seek conversations with strangers. Discuss it all together. (*Note:* Avoid tough neighborhoods.)

Visit restaurants you have never been to before, together. Make a minimum purchase. (The adventure is the thing; plus, you'll know how to use the place in the future).

Go to your local library and read up on particular subjects that each of you enjoys. Then discuss what you learned and your responses.

> **Select unknown towns nearby,** and drive or walk around them.

> **Play a game,** like Scrabble or Monopoly. Small prizes to the winner!

> **Celebrate something**—a national holiday, or a party with mutual friends. Play music, offer wine, enjoy your life!

> **Examine a map of nearby areas, and circle any bridges shown.** Each bridge is likely to be located over some interesting sight. By visiting them, you enter a magical place you've never been before.

Over the course of *our* fun excursions, my wife and I crossed many Manhattan bridges, saw the oddest things, met interesting people, and had a great time. We ended up in a hospital, a police station, fairgrounds, a church, plus other strange places. The hospital was most fascinating!

Chapter 27

Holidays

Always try to make holidays special. Holidays offer you a chance to find out how free time can bring you closer together. After all, virtually every day has its responsibilities, but holidays offer a unique opportunity to indulge yourselves and change your usual routine.

At Easter:

Give her a card that says:

You are MY bunny, honey.	I just love to hop around with you.
Eggs, shmeggs, I love your legs.	Neither North, South, or West will be what you are—my East-er love.
You are my box of Easter chocolates.	You are cuter than any bunny.
Chewing Easter candy is OK, but I prefer a chew on YOU.	You are my honey, bunny.

On President's Day in February, tell her:

You are far superior to Washington or Lincoln to me.	YOU are my President!
Today, darling, you get my vote.	In my book, you hold the highest office in the land.
You have the best Constitution.	A vote for you is a vote for love.
You get an "X" on *my* ballot.	In the next election, you get my vote no matter who is running.

Start the Fourth of July off with a bang, saying:

You are the warmest explosion I've ever known.	You are my July Fourth celebration.
You set my crackers on fire.	It's the fourth of July, and you taste like my favorite pie.
Firecrackers are fine, but darling, please be mine.	BING! BANG! BISS! How about a kiss?
Your fireworks light up my night.	The fireworks last all day and all night with you.

On Valentine's Day

Write a card, put it in an envelope, and leave it near her for her to find. You could write:

I love you.	I adore you.
You are my everything.	You make me a better man.
I love your kisses.	Today, you are everything I want.
You smell delicious.	I just love to look at you.

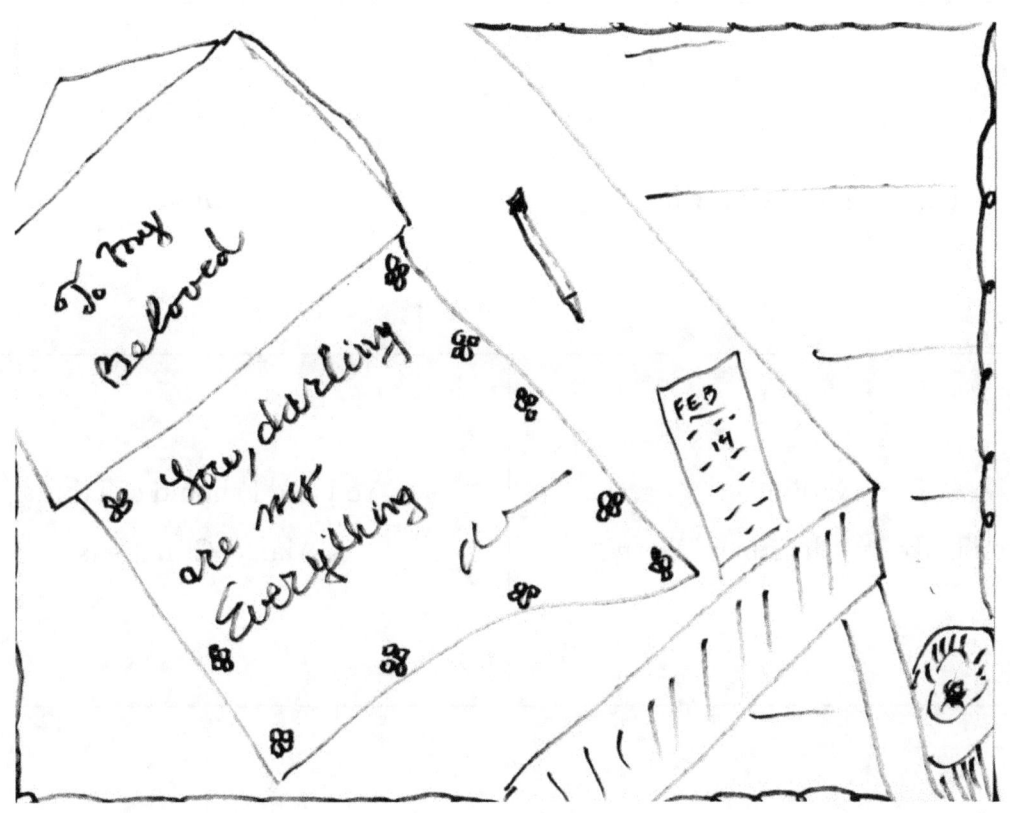

At Christmas or any other similar holiday,

Send her a note (you can adapt it to fit the special holiday you celebrate):

You are my Christmas gift.	You should be wrapped in pretty paper with colorful ribbons and bows.
What can be a better gift than just having you as my wife?	You would be the very best present under the tree.
No gift compares to having you as my wife.	Santa knew exactly what I wanted… YOU!
Darling, you make my Christmas "Merry."	You and I should call this a "Marry" Christmas.

On her birthday:

Go all out!

On your anniversary,

Write a note to her:

I wear my wedding ring with pride.	I'll never forget the day we were wed.
Today, darling, we are one.	You are my favorite love song.
Today, your kisses are the very best.	I'm so happy, sweetheart, that we got married.
Every day with you is Lover's Day.	I love your hugs, especially today.

Conclusion

The object of all these efforts is to increase every man's chance to improve his marriage or relationship. Naturally, you will add your own touches and disregard what won't work for you. I sincerely hope that this kit helps you. Here's wishing you good luck.

If you have really made use of the numerous ideas and suggestions but your mate has rejected your efforts, find someone else.

Acknowledgments

This kit is the result of Terry McConnell's suggestions, editing, and encouragement. He's the man I call "son."

This book would never have been published without the assistance and involvement of Diane Kurinsky and Steve Gross. Without the love, inspiration, and efforts of my incredible daughter-in-law, Diane, it wouldn't even have become a book. She knew what this book meant to me; she cherished the longevity of my loving marriage and what I have contributed to it; and as a psychotherapist, she wanted to help make my wisdom available to other husbands so that they could truly become "happy husbands." So she brought my manuscript to her friend Naomi Rose to transform into a book. Naomi suggested insightful editorial changes, typeset the text and my original drawings, and turned it into the book you have in your hands right now.

About the Author

Just so you know, I'm in my mid-nineties, have excellent health, and work out at the "Y" with much younger people.

World War II drafted me. I served three years in the South Pacific, no holidays. Won five battle stars in that jungle war. Trained as a Radio-Gunner. My outfit was the Fifth Bomber Command.

I worked mostly as sales manager for firms like Mattel, Shop Vac, and the Professional Marketing Association.

Best of all, I married a woman I knew when I was eleven years old, and we've been madly in love all through our many years together.

Oh, one thing I left out: In professional testing, I was told my creative abilities were so unique that there was no grade for me. I received a four-year free college award from Cooper Union College in New York.

And may each one reading this book benefit from my experiences.

www.ingramcontent.com/pod-product-compliance
Lightning Source LLC
Chambersburg PA
CBHW060516300426
44112CB00017B/2699